A MATCH MADE IN SPACE

"You're just not thinking fourth
dimensionally."
—Doc Brown

"If time travel is possible, where are the tourists from the future?"
—Stephen Hawking

"The past is obdurate."
—Stephen King

"Las historias de viaje en el tiempo son demasiado divertidas para ser eliminadas simplemente por consideraciones mundanas sobre impracticabilidad o incluso imposibilidad."
—Isaac Asimov

"History doesn't repeat itself, but it
harmonizes, and what it usually makes
is the devil's music."
—Stephen King

"All moments,
past, present and future,
always have existed,
always will exist."
—Kurt Vonnegut

"PointlesSness is the point."
-James Hunt

Made in the USA
Lexington, KY
26 December 2015